SHAPED BY SCRIPTURE

## Your God Will Be My God

# RUTH
# ESTHER

## C. JEANNE ORJALA SERRÃO

Copyright © 2022 by The Foundry Publishing
The Foundry Publishing®
PO Box 419527
Kansas City, MO 64141
thefoundrypublishing.com

978-0-8341-3935-0

Printed in the
United States of America

Cover and Interior Design: J. R. Caines
Layout: Jeff Gifford

10 9 8 7 6 5 4 3 2 1

# Contents

# THE *SHAPED BY SCRIPTURE* SERIES

The first step of an organized study of the Bible is the selection of a biblical book, which is not always an easy task. Often people pick a book they are already familiar with, books they think will be easy to understand, or books that, according to popular opinion, seem to have more relevance to Christians today than other books of the Bible. However, it is important to recognize the truth that God's Word is not limited to just a few books. All the biblical books, both individually and collectively, communicate God's Word to us. As Paul affirms in 2 Timothy 3:16, "All Scripture is God-breathed and is useful for teaching, rebuking, correcting and training in righteousness." We interpret the term "God-breathed" to mean inspired by God. If Christians are going to take 2 Timothy 3:16 seriously, then we should all set the goal of encountering God's Word as communicated through all sixty-six books of the Bible.

By purchasing this volume, you have chosen to study the Old Testament books of Ruth and Esther. You have a made a great choice because Ruth and Esther teach us about the faithfulness of God, even in difficult situations. They are also the only two books in the Bible named after women. However, do not let that fool you; they have much to teach both women and men! It might interest you to know that the early Jewish readers of these books were all men. Moreover, because men endorsed the ancient sacred texts, the endorsement of these two books for inclusion in the Holy Bible indicates the common understanding and agreement that these stories are important for everyone. The goal of this series is to illustrate an appropriate method of studying the Bible. Since these are short books, they are a perfect size for in-depth Bible study.

# How This Study Works

This Bible study is intended for a period of seven weeks. We have chosen a specific passage for each week's study. This study can be done individually or with a small group.

For individual study, we recommend a five-day study each week, following the guidelines given below:

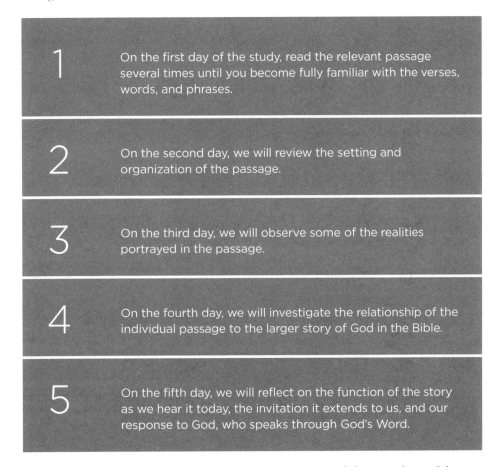

1 — On the first day of the study, read the relevant passage several times until you become fully familiar with the verses, words, and phrases.

2 — On the second day, we will review the setting and organization of the passage.

3 — On the third day, we will observe some of the realities portrayed in the passage.

4 — On the fourth day, we will investigate the relationship of the individual passage to the larger story of God in the Bible.

5 — On the fifth day, we will reflect on the function of the story as we hear it today, the invitation it extends to us, and our response to God, who speaks through God's Word.

If this Bible study is done as a group activity, we recommend that members of the group meet together on the sixth day to share and discuss what they have learned from God's Word and how it has transformed their lives.

You may want to have a study Bible to give you additional insights as we work through the books of Ruth and Esther. Other helpful resources are *Discovering the Old Testament* and *Ruth/Song of Songs/Esther: A Commentary in the Wesleyan Tradition*, available from The Foundry Publishing.

## Literary Forms in the Bible

There are several literary forms represented throughout the Bible. The divinely inspired writers used various techniques to communicate God's Word to their ancient audiences. The major literary forms (also known as genres) of the Bible are:

- narratives

- laws

- history

- Wisdom literature (in the form of dialogues and proverbial statements)

- poetry (consisting of poems of praise, lament, trust in God, and more)

- prophecy

- discourses

- parables

- miracle stories

- letters (also known as epistles)

- exhortations

- apocalyptic writings

Within each of these forms, one may find subgenres. Each volume in the *Shaped by Scripture* series will briefly overview the genres found in the book of the Bible that is the subject of that study.

When biblical writers utilized a particular literary form, they intended for it to have a specific effect on their audience. This concept can be understood by examining genres that are familiar to us in our contemporary setting. For example, novels that are comedies inspire good and happy feelings in their readers; tragedies, on the other hand, are meant to induce sorrow. What is true of the intended effect of literary forms in contemporary literature is also true of literary forms found in the Bible.

# THE BOOKS OF RUTH AND ESTHER

The message of the biblical books, though it originates with God, comes to us through individuals whom God inspired to communicate his word to humanity. They fulfilled their task by utilizing their literary skill as speakers and writers of God's message. This message came to these individuals in particular historical circumstances in the history of God's people — Israel in the Old Testament period and the early Christian church in the New Testament period. In addition, biblical books communicate certain clearly developed understandings about God, humanity, sin, judgment, salvation, human hope, and more. Bible studies should be done with an awareness of the theological themes in a particular book. So, prior to our engagement with Ruth and Esther, we will briefly summarize what we know about these books in general, their authorship, the literary forms, the historical settings behind them, and major theological themes.

## The Writings: Festival Scrolls

Ruth is found in the English Bible right after Judges because the first verse in Ruth says, "In the days when the judges ruled." Esther is found right after Nehemiah because the first verse in Esther says, "This is what happened during the time of Xerxes," indicating that the setting for this story is during the time of Persian rule. Cyrus, the king of Persia, allows the Jews to return to the promised land, but not all the Jews return. Esther is the story of what happens to the Jews who stay in Persia.

In the Hebrew Bible, both of these books are in the section called The Writings (or *Kethubim*), and they are often grouped together with Song of Songs, Ecclesiastes, and Lamentations as the Festal Scrolls (or *Megillot*). This tells us that these books are read during special festival times, recounting the history of what God has done in the lives of his people. Ruth is usually read during the Feast of Weeks (or Shavuot). This festival celebrates the giving of the first covenant in the form of the Ten Commandments on Mount Sinai. Esther is read during the Festival of Purim, which celebrates the deliverance of the Jews in Persia.

## Who Wrote Ruth and Esther?

Neither of these books indicates an author within the text, so the authors are considered to be unknown. This was common for short stories from this period, and they were most likely passed on through oral tradition. Oral tradition during ancient times was serious business, not at all like the games of Telephone or Gossip you might have played as a child. Ancient storytellers had the freedom to color the stories with their own descriptions and emphases, but they had to get the facts right, or they were called out by their peers.

For Ruth, Rabbinic tradition says Samuel wrote it, but most scholars dispute this because the book has the sense of having been written a long time after King David. Since Ruth was David's great-grandmother, the importance of the story is elevated by her connection to Israel's greatest king. Some scholars think a royal scribe seeking to preserve the lineage of King David might have written it. However, this is no boring history of David's family. Therefore, many scholars believe a professional storyteller wrote it, perhaps even a wise woman because the author is especially tuned in to the thoughts and emotions of Ruth and Naomi.

For Esther, scholars have generally disagreed with the Talmudic statements that men of the Great Synagogue wrote it. Other ancient writers have suggested that Mordecai was the author. This is also disputed since the author and Mordecai appear to be different people in Esther 9:26, where the author inserts an explanation to his contemporary audience. Because of the omission of any references to Jerusalem or Judah, many scholars think the author probably lived in northern Persia, perhaps in Susa itself. The most likely scenario is that this book, like Ruth, was written by a professional storyteller—but unlike with Ruth, there is no reason to believe a wise woman wrote it because the emphasis in Esther is on plot and action with little character development.

## Literary Form

Ruth is a classic short story, with a legal narrative related to marriage customs of the period. The story, told from Naomi's point of view, makes Ruth the central figure. The author uses typical forms for oaths and blessings. The oaths intensify promises, like Ruth's promise to follow Naomi in 1:17 and Boaz's promise to redeem (marry) Ruth in 3:13. Ruth 1:9 uses the ancient blessing form, where Naomi blesses Orpah and Ruth when she releases them to return to their families in Moab. The formula blessing is also found in 2:30, when Naomi blesses Boaz for his kindness, and in 4:11, with the wedding blessing by the town.

Esther is also a short story that uses common Jewish poetic forms like parallelism and rhythm but in a narrative account. Although the Hebrew is awkward and the vocabulary minimal, the use of irony is prominent. Esther is rewarded after disobeying the king twice, while Vashti is deposed after one disobedience; we also find Haman describing to the king how to honor Mordecai (his arch enemy) while thinking he himself is the one to be honored. On top of that, Haman is the one the king asks to lead Mordecai through the streets, telling everyone how great Mordecai is!

## Historical Context and Date

The historical settings for these stories are clearly stated in the texts themselves. Ruth 1:1 says the story takes place during the time of the judges. As we know from Scripture, "the time of the judges" fluctuated in stability when it came to the safety and well-being of the Israelites. Naomi's family move to Moab to find a place where the famine is not so severe, indicating that individual families feel the need and freedom to go elsewhere for their own food security and safety needs. It is not a time when a king can come to their rescue or organize to meet the needs of his subjects.

Esther 1:1 says the story takes place under the reign of King Xerxes, during the rule of the Persian Empire. Since Xerxes I began his rule about forty-five years after Cyrus the Great died, this is a story about the Jews who stayed in Persia after Cyrus gave them the opportunity to return to Israel to rebuild Jerusalem and the temple. The conditions for the Persia-remaining Jews indicate vulnerability due to their ethnicity and religion. Note that Mordecai initially tells Esther not to reveal her Jewish ancestry to the king or anyone in the court. Esther's bravery in the face of this vulnerability is amazing.

When it comes to when the stories were written down or considered to be part of the biblical canon, the dates are much later and more debated. For Ruth, the date ranges from the 900s to the 300s BC. A date in the 800s coincides with Jehoshaphat's reform that included the idea of care for the outcasts. Perhaps the story also argues for the value of mixed marriages, validating Solomon's marriages to gentiles.

For Esther, the dating is more complicated. Scholars say the date has to deal with the first form and final form of the book. Most scholars agree that the final form of Esther took shape in the 100s BC, even though we do not find it among the Qumran Dead Sea Scrolls. The earliest date for its initial composition is around 400 BC, which suggests the institution of the Purim Festival tradition. The 100s date would remind the Jews of God's deliverance in Persia at a time when the Jews were under Syrian domination, moving into the Maccabean dynasty period.

## Literary Structure

Both Esther and Ruth are whole narratives whose goal is to tell a story. One can divide Ruth into four sections that follow the four chapters, with a genealogy tacked on to the end of the story. Some scholars divide the story into only two parts, reflecting primarily the locations where the story takes place. We will follow the chapter divisions in this study.

Most scholars divide the ten chapters of Esther into thirteen sections, which we will combine into five sections of two chapters each.

## Major Theological Themes

The major theological themes in Ruth are all related to God's love in action.

 *Hesed*, **the Hebrew word for "faithful love," is found in Ruth's love for Naomi, Boaz's love for Ruth, and God's love for those in need.** This rich word describes the love of God that is meant to be given to all people. Actions express this kind of love, not just words.

 **God works behind the scenes through those who are faithful to him.** Rarely does God work through direct intervention. In Ruth, the events appear to be coincidental, but the author and the reader know better—it is the providence of God.

 **Redemption, a word used twenty-three times in Ruth's four chapters, is key.** Although it has specific reference to responsibilities of levirate marriages (a brother or close relative marrying a widow to continue the family line and provide for the widow), it also encompasses the idea of salvation. As an expression of *hesed*, it has a practical meaning of love expressed through caring and faithful action.

In Esther, God is never mentioned at all, but that does not mean the author of Esther and the characters in this book are not keenly aware of God's presence and providence. Some of the theological themes in Esther revolve around God's seeming hiddenness.

**Although Esther is one of only two books in the entire Bible that do not use a word for God, God's presence and faithfulness are found in God's deliverance of his people.** The exodus was *the* formative deliverance of the Jewish people, and the book of Esther describes God's continuing faithfulness to deliver his people even as they remain in a foreign nation.

**As in Ruth, we find the providence of God at work and recognized in this book.** The events seem to be coincidences and a fortunate series of events, including: the choosing of Esther to be queen out of many beautiful women in the empire, the favor of the king to grant Esther's desires, and the king's recollection that Mordecai saved his life. However, the author and readers know God was behind it all.

**We also see the movement in theological understanding by the Jewish people that God is present with them even when they choose not to live in the promised land.** Their nature as Jews and their relationship with God is spiritual and transcends the confines of a physical place.

**God can bring about reversals of life circumstances for his people.** As Jesus later says in the Gospels, the first shall be last and the last, first. Esther is full of examples of how God turns a scary and horrible situation into a blessing. The use of irony throughout the book describes these reversals.

# RUTH 1-2

Our purpose in studying the first two chapters in Ruth is to see how God's providence works out in the family of Elimelek. Although Elimelek makes the decision to leave Bethlehem in Judea to move to Moab, with its own gods and customs, to escape the famine and economic depression of Judea, the move proves costly for the family. Elimelek and both of his sons die, leaving the women (Naomi and her childless daughters-in-law) destitute. The family is without heirs and in worse shape than when they left Bethlehem.

Naomi realizes it would be better for her to return to her relatives because they will have an obligation to care for her. Because her Moabite daughters-in-law do not have children, they are no longer legally bound to Elimelek's family and can go home to be cared for by their families and perhaps get married again and have children of their own.

Ruth's love for Naomi (including Naomi's God and Naomi's culture) results in her determination to go with Naomi back to Bethlehem. Here we see that moving away from God's people has resulted in catastrophe, but when Naomi returns to her people, she blesses Ruth and brings her into the circle of God's people. It is Ruth's decision, but it results in the redemption of the entire Elimelek family through her.

## WEEK 1, DAY 1

Listen to the passage in Ruth 1–2 by reading it aloud several times until you become familiar with its verses, words, and phrases. Enjoy the experience of imagining the story in your mind, picturing each event as it unfolds.

# WEEK 1, DAY 21

## The Setting

It is customary to begin the study of a biblical passage by asking questions about its historical, cultural, religious, and literary setting. The story of Ruth is set during the time of the Israelite judges, so it is a time of food and safety insecurity as well as increasing violence (see Judges 17–21). There is no strong central government, as will exist later during the monarchy.

Ruth comes from the Moabite people, who live east of the Jordan River, beyond the Dead Sea. Although they were originally of the same ethnic background, Moab (son of Lot, Abraham's nephew) was born from incest (Genesis 19:30–38), so the Israelite relationship with Moab is full of sexual and idolatry issues. The Moabites' national god is Chemosh in the same way that Yahweh is the God of the Israelites. The extreme Israelite abhorrence of the Moabites at this time indicates that life in Bethlehem, where Naomi's family comes from, is so bad that even idolatrous Moab seems a better place to live! Likewise, for Ruth, moving to Bethlehem from Moab would subject her to discrimination and injustice without the protection of Naomi and, later, Boaz.

Bethlehem is about six miles south of Jerusalem, on the edge of the part of the land with sustainable rainfall. These conditions lead to frequent famines that plague that part of Israel. The main economy is farming and herding sheep and goats, which obviously depends on adequate rainfall. Bethlehem is the location of Rachel's tomb and, later, the city of David's birth.

The traditional date for the writing of Ruth varies between the tenth to the fourth century BC, indicating that the story was written down to show the diversity in the line of Israel's greatest king, David. One of the purposes of the book is to widen the circle of people who have the moral ability to become worshipers of Yahweh.

## The Plot

To discover the plot of Ruth 1–2, let us look at the structure of these chapters. The story begins with why Elimelek and his family have to leave Bethlehem for Moab and what happens to the family in Moab. It continues with Naomi and Ruth returning to Bethlehem, and ends with Ruth meeting Boaz in his harvest field.

For the purpose of our study, we will divide this passage into nine sections. Let us examine each of those sections. **Below, write down next to each grouping of verses the main theme the verses report (following the pattern provided).**

### 1. Ruth 1:1–5

Elimelek, an Ephrathite from Bethlehem leaves his home with his wife and two sons to live in

Moab because of famine in Bethlehem. Elimelek dies in Moab, leaving his wife, Naomi, and her

two sons. They marry Moabite women, but after ten years, the sons also die.

### 2. Ruth 1:6–14

### 3. Ruth 1:15–18

### 4. Ruth 1:19–22

### 5. Ruth 2:1–3

## 6. Ruth 2:4–7

_____

_____

_____

_____

_____

_____

## 7. Ruth 2:8–13

_____

_____

_____

_____

_____

_____

## 8. Ruth 2:14–20

_____

_____

_____

_____

_____

_____

## 9. Ruth 2:21–23

Boaz invites Ruth to glean until the end of the harvest season. Naomi encourages Ruth to do this for both economic and safety reasons. Ruth finishes the harvest in Boaz's field, staying close to the women harvesters and living with Naomi.

**WORD STUDY NOTES #1**

[1] Ephrathite and Ephraimite both come from the same Hebrew word, identifying Elimelek as a descendant of Ephraim the son of Joseph. This means Elimelek is from the tribe of Joseph.

[2] Moab is a few miles east of Bethlehem in the mountainous area east of the Dead Sea. While the people there are from the same family as Abraham, they have, by this time, developed a different culture and religion. Their language is a dialect of Hebrew, so communication is possible.

[3] A widow in the ancient Mediterranean culture was dependent on her sons, or other male relatives, for interaction with the public world and for living support. When Naomi's sons die, she is in a critical situation because she has no other male relatives in Moab.

**WORD STUDY NOTES #2**

[1] Because Ruth and Orpah do not have children, they are no longer considered part of Naomi's family, so they can easily go back to their own families and perhaps be married again to other husbands and bear children.

[2] What Naomi is referencing in verses 12-13 is the levirate custom in which a brother or close male relative marries a widow and reproduces in the name of his brother/relative so that the family line goes on.

# WEEK 1, DAY 3

## What's Happening in the Story?

As we notice certain circumstances in the story, we will begin to see how they are similar to or different from the realities of our world. The story will become the lens through which we see the world in which we live today. In our study today, you may encounter words and/or phrases that are unfamiliar to you. Some of the particular words and translation choices for them have been explained in more detail in the **Word Study Notes**. If you are interested in even more help or detail, you can supplement this study with a Bible dictionary or other Bible study resources.

### 1. Ruth 1:1–5

Ruth begins with identifying Elimelek as an Ephrathite[1] who moves from his home in Bethlehem to the land of Moab[2] with his wife and two sons. The reason for the move is a famine in Bethlehem, and they are only moving there for a while until things improve in Bethlehem. Elimelek dies while they are in Moab, leaving Naomi and her two sons. The sons marry Moabite women and settle in to live in Moab. After ten years, both sons die, and Naomi becomes a widow with no means of support.[3] Her situation is now worse than if they had stayed in Bethlehem.

**Practice the above pattern to jot down a summary description of the reality portrayed in Ruth 1:6–14.**

### 2. Ruth 1:6–14[1, 2]

_____

_____

_____

_____

_____

_____

_____

### 3. Ruth 1:15–18

Orpah decides to go back home, but Ruth is so devoted to Naomi that she confesses her belief in the God of Israel and swears an oath to intensify her intention of becoming all she needs to be to go to Bethlehem and become part of Naomi's family, people, and religion.

### 4. Ruth 1:19–22

Naomi and Ruth are welcomed in Bethlehem, and Naomi confesses that she left Bethlehem full but has returned empty and bitter. The decision of the family to leave their land was a very costly one, and Naomi is returning devastated.

**Create your own brief description of the world and reality portrayed in Ruth 2:1–3.**

### 5. Ruth 2:1–3[1]

_____

_____

_____

_____

_____

_____

**WORD STUDY NOTES #5**

[1] At this time, the desperately poor are allowed to follow the harvesters to pick up any grain that falls along the edges of the fields. It is a kind of welfare system for the poor.

17

### 6. Ruth 2:4–7

Boaz arrives at the field and notices Ruth. He finds out she is the Moabite daughter-in-law of Naomi and that she has asked to gather grain behind the harvesters. She has not asked for more privileges than any other poor person, and she is a hard worker.

**Write your own brief description of the world and reality portrayed in Ruth 2:8–13 and 14–20.**

_____

_____

_____

## 7. Ruth 2:8–13[1]

_____

_____

_____

_____

_____

_____

_____

_____

_____

_____

_____

## 8. Ruth 2:14–20[1]

_____

_____

_____

_____

_____

_____

_____

_____

_____

_____

## 9. Ruth 2:21–23

Boaz extends his one-day generosity and protection to the whole harvest season. Naomi and Ruth's lives are secure and even abundant!

## Discoveries

Let's summarize our discoveries from Ruth 1-2.

1. It is often better to stay and face the problems we have, trusting God to take care of us, then to take things into our own hands and try to solve them ourselves.

2. We have to do the right thing, even if it is hard and causes us emotional distress. Right does not mean easy and safe.

3. God recognizes and rewards faithful devotion, whether to God or to the welfare of another person.

4. When we trust God, his blessings do not only meet our needs but also give us abundant life.

5. There are real dangers in the world because of sin, and God expects us to use our reason and not intentionally put ourselves in situations where we can be hurt.

19

# WEEK 1, DAY 4

If you have a study Bible, it may have references in a margin, a middle column, or footnotes that point to other biblical texts. You may find it helpful in understanding how the whole story of God ties together to look up some of those other scriptures from time to time.

## Living Faithfully and the Story of God

Whenever we read a biblical text, it is important to ask how the particular text we are reading relates to the rest of the Bible. We can find the themes of living faithfully in the generosity and protection of God in other places. **In the space provided, write a short summary of how the faithfulness and generosity themes are utilized in each passage.**

**1. Deuteronomy 15:1–11**

_____

_____

_____

_____

_____

_____

_____

_____

**2. Psalm 105**

_____

_____

_____

_____

_____

_____

_____

_____

_____

_____

**3. Psalm 132**

**4. Isaiah 55:1–7**

**5. Matthew 6:25–32**

**6. 2 Corinthians 9:6–15**

_____
_____
_____
_____
_____
_____
_____
_____
_____

**7. 1 Timothy 6:17–19**

_____
_____
_____
_____
_____
_____
_____
_____
_____

**8. Hebrews 11:1–16**

_____
_____
_____
_____
_____
_____
_____
_____
_____

# WEEK 1, DAY 5

## Ruth and Our World Today

When we look at the themes of faithfulness and generosity in Ruth, these themes can become the lens through which we see ourselves, our world, and how God works in our world today.

**1. What does Ruth's determination and faithful love for Naomi, Naomi's people, and Naomi's God say to us about our world, God's action in our world today, and ourselves?**

God is faithful to us as we determine to be faithful to God and God's direction in our lives. Living a faithful life of integrity is not for the fainthearted.

Following the above example, answer these questions about how we can understand our world, God's action, and ourselves in our world today.

**2. What do you observe about the ways God blesses those around you who have gone through difficult times?**

**3. We are to trust God in all situations. How does the guidance from both Naomi and Boaz for Ruth to stay with the women harvesters and avoid being alone help us to see how reason and trust work together?**

**4.** These passages in Ruth remind us that faithfulness to God brings about abundant blessings in our lives. What is the attitude of our world about this way of life? How does that affect us?

_____

_____

_____

_____

_____

**5.** Elimelek chooses to leave his country because of the famine in Bethlehem, rather than trust God to take care of his family. How hard is it for us to trust God rather than try to solve our own problems?

_____

_____

_____

_____

_____

## Invitation and Response

God's Word always invites a response. Think about the way these themes of faithfulness and generosity speak to us today. How do they invite us to respond?

Ruth's story invites us to consider the ways that we could be faithful in our ordinary, everyday lives in places where we might think it's least important. It also invites us to consider how we—God's own people—can embody the presence of God for the sake of offering life and security to vulnerable people.

What is your evaluation of yourself based on what we've learned from Ruth 1 and 2?

_____

_____

_____

_____

_____

Ruth's decision results in the redemption of the entire Elimelek family through her.

# RUTH 3-4

The purpose of our study of Ruth 3–4 is to discover the roles of holy boldness and love in action. In these chapters, we find Naomi, Ruth, and Boaz all boldly carrying out actions that they perceive to be right. This boldness comes from their love for one another that is characterized by action and relationship.

---

## WEEK 2, DAY 1

Listen to the passage in Ruth 3–4 by reading it aloud several times until you become familiar with its verses, words, and phrases. Enjoy the twists and turns of these chapters as the three main characters boldly go about caring for each other with love in action.

# WEEK 2, DAY 2

## RUTH 3-4

## The Setting

These chapters contain the plans for Naomi to secure Ruth's future and plans for Ruth and Boaz to secure Naomi's future. Naomi's love for Ruth results in a bold plan for Ruth to secure the attention of Boaz in a way that conveys to him that he should marry Ruth. The plan and the story are full of sexual innuendo and tension that can be misunderstood by contemporary Christian standards but were appropriate and acceptable in the customs of the time. The community refers to both Boaz and Ruth as people of worth or high moral standing. On Day 3, we will discuss some of the specific cultural phrases and terms. It is important to know that ancient Israelite marriage began with engagement, and sexual relations often began before the official week of marriage celebrations.

Ruth obeys Naomi's instructions but also adds to them in her requests to Boaz on the threshing floor. She not only presents herself as a viable wife for him but also asks that, as a relative of Naomi's family, he redeem her land and secure her future. Boaz agrees to both requests from Ruth and sends Ruth back to Naomi without announcing their engagement to others on the threshing floor. He has a plan to persuade the other close relative, who should already be looking after Naomi but has not been, to give up his right to the inheritance of Elimelek's land.

Boaz calls elders from the city together and publicly confronts the unnamed relative and ties the inheritance with the duty of providing an heir to go with the inherited land. Strictly speaking, the providing of an heir to carry on the name of Elimelek is not required since the closest male relative inherits the property. However, Boaz appeals publicly to the justice and morality of providing for these widowed women to coerce the relative into giving up his claims to the property. The sandals ceremony legalizes the agreement, and—as all good stories end—the rest is history!

## The Plot

To discover the message of Ruth 3–4, let us look at the way the writer has structured the plot. The author begins by describing Naomi's unselfish desire to secure Ruth's future because Ruth will be even more vulnerable if Naomi should suddenly die. Then Ruth's love for Naomi results in her bold request of Boaz to secure Naomi's future. Boaz's love for Ruth results in his bold and public negotiations to secure both their futures, and gain Ruth as his wife. What we learn here is that real love always results in actions to secure the well-being of the loved one. Love is more than talk and often results in bold action, especially where injustice is concerned.

For the purpose of our study, we will divide this passage into eight sections. Let us examine each of those sections. **Below, write down next to each grouping of verses the main theme the verses report following the examples provided.**

### 1. Ruth 3:1-9

Naomi is concerned about finding a secure future for Ruth, so she puts a plan together to get Ruth noticed by Boaz. Naomi's bold plan asks Ruth to risk everything in asking Boaz to marry her, using the customs of the day. Ruth does everything Naomi tells her to do.

### 2. Ruth 3:10-15

### 3. Ruth 3:16-18

## 4. Ruth 4:1–8

## 5. Ruth 4:9–10

Boaz calls the ten elders as witnesses to his purchase of Naomi's family land  and announces his marriage to Ruth.

## 6. Ruth 4:11-12

## 7. Ruth 4:13–17

## 8. Ruth 4:18–22

The author of Ruth closes the book with a genealogy that establishes Obed (Boaz + Ruth's son) as part of a prestigious Israelite family line that eventually produces the esteemed King David.

## What's Happening in the Story?

As we notice certain circumstances in the story, we will begin to see how they are similar to or different from the realities of our world. The story will become the lens through which we see the world in which we live today. In our study today, you may encounter words and/or phrases that are unfamiliar to you. Some of the particular words and translation choices for them have been explained in more detail in the **Word Study Notes**. If you are interested in even more help or detail, you can supplement this study with a Bible dictionary or other Bible study resources.

### 1. Ruth 3:1–9

Naomi wants to find a husband for Ruth so that, when Naomi dies, Ruth will have a future in Bethlehem. She has chosen Boaz because he is a relative[1] and has already extended kindness to Ruth and Naomi in allowing her to glean in his harvest field. She tells Ruth to wash and perfume herself and wrap herself in a coat or cloak. Ruth is to keep herself hidden from Boaz until after he has finished eating and drinking at the threshing floor. When Boaz lies down to sleep, Ruth is to take note of where he is and wait until the middle of the night to approach him. Then she is to uncover his private parts and lie down beside him.[2] Finally, Naomi directs Ruth to do whatever Boaz tells her to do. When Boaz is finished eating and drinking he lies down in a private area of the threshing floor, behind the grain pile.[3] Ruth quietly uncovers his private parts and lies down beside him. In the middle of the night, he discovers Ruth lying next to him, and when he asks who she is, she tells him that she is his servant[4] and that he should spread his clothes over her since he is a marriageable relative.[5]

**WORD STUDY NOTES #1**

[1] During this Israelite era, Israelites prefer to keep their women close by marrying within the extended family. Sons can marry outside the family and bring those women into the extended family. We see these strategies both here and in the marrying of Naomi's sons to Moabite women.

[2] This passage is charged with sexual tension because Naomi uses the term "to lie with," which can simply mean to lie beside someone, but it can also mean "to lie with sexually." The text says "uncover his feet," which is a euphemism for his private parts.

[3] We can only speculate on why Boaz sleeps on the threshing floor during this community harvest celebration, but it is obviously the custom since Naomi expects him to sleep there.

[4] Ruth uses a subordinate term to refer to herself ("servant") but not the lowest form of servant that would make her ineligible to be Boaz's wife.

[5] Ruth suggests marriage by asking Boaz to extend his clothing to cover her. Boaz's acceptance of her requests signifies his commitment to marrying her. Many scholars see this as their engagement.

**Practice the previous pattern to jot down a summary description of the reality that is portrayed in Ruth 3:10–15.**

## 2. Ruth 3:10–15[1]

_____

_____

_____

_____

_____

## 3. Ruth 3:16–18

Ruth returns home, and Naomi asks her how it went. Ruth tells her everything and gives her the six measures of barley, indicating that Boaz intended them for Naomi. Naomi realizes that Boaz is sincere and eager to marry Ruth,[1] so she tells Ruth to wait for his next moves. She is sure Boaz would settle the issue that day.

## 4. Ruth 4:1-6

Boaz immediately goes to the gate of the city[1] to wait for the close relative who has rights to Naomi's land before Boaz.[2] When he comes to the gate, he invites this relative to sit down with him. Then he asks ten of the elders of the town who are there at the gate to come over and sit with them. Boaz explains the situation to the other relative and asks if he plans to redeem Naomi's piece of land, and informs the relative that he, Boaz, intends to redeem it as next in line if this man does not.[3] The man says he will redeem it, but Boaz isn't finished. Boaz adds the moral responsibility of acquiring Ruth, the Moabitess, so that the name of the deceased (Elimelek and his sons) will follow the inherited land. With this added responsibility, the kinsman-redeemer rescinds his promise to buy the land because he cannot afford the additional obligation, and gives Boaz the right to buy the land and acquire Ruth.

**WORD STUDY NOTES #2**

[1] Boaz is not the closest relative who would inherit Naomi's land, so Boaz cannot fulfill Ruth's second request for buying Naomi's land to give her the money to live on. However, he has a plan to make this happen.

**WORD STUDY NOTES #3**

[1] What happened between Boaz and Ruth and the promises made make it obvious to Naomi that Boaz has agreed to marry Ruth. The gift of barley is considered by some scholars to be a kind of bride-price for Ruth. Therefore, this gift would also be indicative that an engagement took place that night.

**WORD STUDY NOTES #4**

[1] The gate to ancient cities is like the center of social and commercial activity. This is where the market stalls are and where business and legal transactions take place publicly.

[2] Boaz needs the city elders to recognize his request, so this is the place for this legal action to take place.

[3] What Boaz is really doing here is calling out the relative for being lax in his responsibility as a kinsman-redeemer. He should have already bought Naomi's land so she would have money to live on for the rest of her life.

**Write your own brief description of the world and reality portrayed in Ruth 4:7–8 and 9–10.**

## 5. Ruth 4:7–8

_____

_____

_____

_____

_____

_____

_____

## 6. Ruth 4:9–10

_____

_____

_____

_____

_____

_____

_____

**WORD STUDY NOTES #7**

[1] The references to Rachel and Leah indicate a blessing of fertility on Boaz and Ruth.

[2] The reference to Perez probably is an indication that Boaz will replace Elimelek in the family line of his future son, Obed, as well as in the family line of King David.

## 7. Ruth 4:11–12

The elders and all the people at the gate confirm their witness to these transactions and bless the marriage of Boaz and Ruth. They ask God to bless Ruth so that she, like Rachel and Leah, will build up the house of Israel[1] and that Boaz will increase his honor in Bethlehem through the child born to Boaz and Ruth, like Perez, who was the son born of the levirate marriage of Tamar.[2]

**Write your own brief description of the world and reality portrayed in Ruth 4:13–17.**

## 8. Ruth 4:13–17[1, 2]

_____

_____

_____

_____

_____

_____

_____

_____

_____

_____

_____

**WORD STUDY NOTES #8**

[1] The birth of Obed is special to Ruth and Boaz, but it is especially important to Naomi because her family line will continue.

[2] The statement to Naomi that Ruth is better than seven sons is the highest compliment of Ruth's devotion to Naomi. Sons, of course, are the natural way for the family line to be extended, and the number seven stands for perfection. So Ruth is better than the perfect son to Naomi!

## 9. Ruth 4:18–22

This is the genealogy starting with Perez, who supplanted his older twin in the family line, and ending with King David. Here Boaz supplants Elimelek and Mahlon in the line of David. Ruth is known for being the great-grandmother of King David!

_____

_____

_____

_____

_____

_____

_____

_____

_____

## Discoveries

Let's summarize our discoveries from Ruth 3–4.

1. Boldness is something God can use to achieve his plans for his people.

2. Sexuality is not a taboo topic in the Bible and is used to bring about God's purpose in the lives of his people.

3. Women in ancient Israel had little by way of prestige and resources to get the things they need. Therefore, they used their sexuality as one of those resources. Ruth is praised for her use of this resource.

4. God can give us the courage to push the boundaries of this sinful world to bring about the salvation of his people.

5. The life of faith is always expressed in one's relationships with others.

6. The love we have for others does not always coincide with what is convenient or proper for us.

7. Love that fills our emptiness does not care about public opinion but presses on to meet the needs of the loved one.

# WEEK 2, DAY 4

## Love in Action and the Story of God

Whenever we read a biblical text, it is important to ask how the particular text we are reading relates to the rest of the Bible. The themes of boldness and love in action have an important place in the story of God. We find these themes in several places in the Bible and in a variety of contexts. In the Old and New Testaments, the themes of boldness and love in action are common. **In the space provided, write a short summary of how the themes of boldness and love in action are utilized in each passage.**

**1. Leviticus 19:18, 34**

_____

_____

_____

_____

_____

_____

_____

**2. Deuteronomy 31:1–8**

_____

_____

_____

_____

_____

_____

_____

If you have a study Bible, it may have references in a margin, a middle column, or footnotes that point to other biblical texts. You may find it helpful in understanding how the whole story of God ties together to look up some of those other scriptures from time to time.

**3. Proverbs 28:1**

**4. Isaiah 56:1–8**

**5. Acts 4:23–31**

**6. Romans 12:9-21**

_____
_____
_____
_____
_____
_____
_____
_____
_____
_____

**7. 1 Corinthians 13**

_____
_____
_____
_____
_____
_____
_____
_____
_____

**8. 1 Corinthians 16:13**

_____
_____
_____
_____
_____
_____
_____
_____

# WEEK 2, DAY 5

## Ruth and Our World Today

When we look at the themes of boldness and love in action in Ruth, these themes can become the lens through which we see ourselves, our world, and how God works in our world today.

**1. How does understanding that Christian boldness comes from God affect how we see our world, God's action, and ourselves in our world today?**

*Many situations and conditions do not bring about God's love and justice in this world. Understanding this and realizing that God wants justice can embolden us to fight for others so they have the justice God wants for them. Our boldness does not come from ourselves. The Holy Spirit gives us boldness, just as it was given to the early disciples after Jesus's ascension.*

Following the above example, answer these questions about how we can understand ourselves, our world, and God's action in our world today.

**2. What do you observe about the nature of love as the world sees it, in contrast with how Jesus talks about love?**

_____

_____

_____

**3. We want to be bold to proclaim the message of the gospel like Peter and John. How do we do this in our modern world?**

_____

_____

_____

**4. The Bible teaches us that the love God gives us is one that results in loving actions. What outward actions define you and your friends as loving Christians?**

_____

_____

_____

_____

**5. Describe a situation where you felt that you acted boldly in Jesus's name. What was the motivation, and what was the response of those around you?**

_____

_____

_____

_____

_____

## Invitation and Response

God's Word always invites a response. Think about the way these themes of boldness and love speak to us today. How do they invite us to respond?

Ruth's story invites us to consider the ways that we are privileged and powerful, like Boaz, and can therefore help those who are more vulnerable. We are also invited to consider the ways we are not privileged or powerful, and how even the humblest follower of God can act boldly in faith and, with God's help, be empowered to change life circumstances for ourselves or someone else.

_____

_____

_____

_____

_____

What is your evaluation of yourself based on what we've learned from Ruth 3–4?

_____

_____

_____

_____

_____

_____

> Love often results in
> bold action, especially
> where injustice
> is concerned.

# ESTHER 1-2

In Esther 1–2 the Persians will teach us how *not* to live, and we will also discuss the importance of concern for the marginalized and learning to love our enemies. In chapter 1, the author describes the decadence and wickedness of the Persian Empire, where some Jews have chosen to live. We also see the marginalization of Queen Vashti, who does nothing other than assert her human right to say no, highlighting the evil of men's oppression of women. In chapter 2, we see Mordecai's response to hearing a plan to kill the king, his enemy. Instead of keeping quiet, he tells Esther, who tells the king, illustrating the command of Christ that will come so many years later—to love our enemies.

## WEEK 3, DAY 1

Listen to the passage in Esther 1–2 by reading it aloud several times until you become familiar with its verses, words, and phrases. Listen to the observations and concerns of the author as he summarizes his story for his readers. How does he treat the themes of concern for the marginalized and godly love of enemies?

## The Setting

This passage begins the story of Esther, who becomes a Jewish queen in the pagan Persian Empire. The story opens with a description of the decadence of the Persian court, where they make decisions around a banquet table that includes much drunkenness. When Queen Vashti defies the king and does not present herself to the drunken mob of men in the king's court, we see the priority for maintaining the oppression of women, expressed by the king's advisors. Queen Vashti is deposed, and an edict is sent out to all the empire that "every man should be ruler over his own household" (1:22).

This leads to the opening for Esther to be selected as the next queen. Esther and the other beautiful virgins are taken, and are subject to beauty treatments and sexual relations with the king at his command. The language suggests that the women have no choice. Esther's character and beauty result in her charming the king, and he crowns her the new queen. We should not read this to mean that the king commits to loving her, but her position in the empire is perhaps better than what might be expected. She has charmed the king, and he is inclined to give her what she desires.

With Esther's position established, the author turns to Mordecai, Esther's uncle, revealing his godly character by reporting to Esther a plot against the king's life. Four hundred years later Jesus will give the command to love one's enemies.

## The Plot

To discover the plot of Esther 1–2, let us look at the way the writer structures the passage. The author begins by describing the world in which Esther will be living. He shows the vulnerability of women in this context by describing the deposing of Queen Vashti and the ensuing edict that men are the rulers of their households. He describes the selection process for the new queen. After the king selects Esther, the author introduces Mordecai as a godly man, in contrast to the Persian court.

For the purpose of our study, we divide this passage into eight sections. Let us examine each of those eight sections. **Below, write down next to each grouping of verses the main theme the verses report, following the examples provided.**

## 1. Esther 1:1–9

King Xerxes is the ruler of a huge empire, including all the lands of the Medes and Persians. The story begins with a great banquet for his military leaders, princes, and nobles that lasts 180 days. The purpose of the banquet is to display his wealth, splendor, and glory. A second banquet begins right after the first, for all the men who live in the citadel (or, walled city) of Susa, including commoners. Lavish descriptions of the decor, couches, and wine goblets are followed by the statement that men can drink of the king's wine as much as they wish. Queen Vashti also gives a banquet at the same time for all the women.

## 2. Esther 1:10–12

## 3. Esther 1:13–20

## 4. Esther 1:21–22

## 5. Esther 2:1–4

_____

_____

_____

_____

_____

_____

_____

## 6. Esther 2:5–11

_____

_____

_____

_____

_____

_____

_____

## 7. Esther 2:12–18

_____

_____

_____

_____

_____

_____

_____

## 8. Esther 2:19–23

One day when Mordecai is sitting by the king's gate, he hears of a plot by two of the king's officials to kill the king. He tells Queen Esther about it, who reports it to the king, giving credit to Mordecai. The plot is investigated, the culprits hanged, and the whole event recorded in the king's records.

# WEEK 3, DAY 3

## What's Happening in the Story?

As we notice certain circumstances in the story, we will begin to see how they are similar to or different from the realities of our world. The story will become the lens through which we see the world in which we live today. In our study today, you may encounter words and/or phrases that are unfamiliar to you. Some of the particular words and translation choices for them have been explained in more detail in the **Word Study Notes**. If you are interested in even more help or detail, you can supplement this study with a Bible dictionary or other Bible study resources.

## 1. Esther 1:1–9

The book of Esther opens by describing the vast kingdom of Xerxes, emphasizing his great authority over the entire known world at that time. He is giving a banquet that lasts 180 days to show his wealth and splendor to all the military leaders, princes, and nobles of all the provinces.[1] Another banquet follows, just for the inhabitants of the citadel of Susa, including both nobles as well as commoners.[2] It lasts only seven days but is no less impressive. The king gives the guest unlimited access to his expensive wine, indicating again a kind of abundant wealth that is beyond imagination. At the same time, in another part of the palace, Queen Vashti is giving her own banquet for the women.

45

**WORD STUDY NOTES #1**

[1] The Hebrew term *hêl* can be translated as the army of Persia and Media, probably officers, indicating this might be a war council for launching an offensive against an enemy. However, *hêl* can also be translated as "the aristocracy," or "wealthy landowners," perhaps indicating the wedding feast celebrating the union of King Xerxes and Queen Vashti.

[2] The citadel is the walled fortress of the city, so it includes those who serve the palace and the king most directly.

## 2. Esther 1:10–12

The king wants to show off his beautiful queen as a continuation of his display of wealth and power. He sends a message via seven eunuchs[1] to command Queen Vashti to come to the men's banquet to show off her beauty. She declines the king's command. The text does not say why, but anyone can guess the possible humiliation of being at the mercy of a mob of drunken men.

**WORD STUDY NOTES #2**

[1] Eunuchs are castrated men who serve the king, particularly in matters relating to the opposite sex.

**Practice the previous pattern to jot down a summary description of the reality that is portrayed in Esther 1:13–22.**

## 3. Esther 1:13–22

_____

_____

_____

_____

_____

_____

_____

_____

_____

_____

_____

_____

_____

_____

_____

_____

_____

_____

## 4. Esther 2:1–4

Later the king's anger subsides, and he begins to miss his wife. To cheer him up, his personal attendants suggest a search of all the most beautiful virgins in all the provinces to be brought into the harem in the citadel of Susa. They also suggest that they be placed under the care of Hegai, the king's eunuch, and be given beauty treatments. Then the king can select from them a new queen to replace Vashti. The king likes this idea and issues orders for it to be done. Again, we see orders being given to appease the personal desires of the king.

**Create your own brief description of the world/reality portrayed in Esther 2:5–11 and Esther 2:12–18.**

## 5. Esther 2:5–11[1]

_____
_____
_____
_____
_____
_____
_____
_____
_____
_____

**WORD STUDY NOTES #5**

[1] The passage uses a series of passive verbs to show that Esther and the other women gathered from the provinces do not have any say over how they are treated or whether they will participate in the process.

## 6. Esther 2:12–18[1]

_____
_____
_____
_____
_____
_____
_____
_____
_____

**WORD STUDY NOTES #6**

[1] For the king to declare a holiday means a period of rest and may perhaps involve relief from taxes, or amnesty.

## 7. Esther 2:19–23

While sitting at the king's gate, Mordecai overhears a plot to assassinate the king. Although the king has taken his adopted daughter and not shown any kindness toward Mordecai, he chooses to love his enemies by warning the king through Queen Esther. After the plot is investigated, the two officials are hanged, and the whole event is recorded in the king's official records.

## Discoveries

Let's summarize our discoveries from Esther 1–2.

1. The description of the Persian court teaches us how not to live. Their excess, pride, and arrogance are not characteristics of God's children, who are to love God with our whole being and love our neighbors as ourselves.

2. The first edict of the king, communicated in response to Queen Vashti's refusal, maintains the fallen social order of the Persian empire, silencing and oppressing women and empowering men to do whatever they want with marginalized women. The gospel teaches us to empower the marginalized and bring justice to the oppressed.

3. Both Judaism and Christianity have historically stood with the marginalized, realizing that God has mercy on the powerless, and so should we.

4. Sexual purity is possible when people have control over their own bodies.

5. With God, we can overcome even the direst circumstances that are totally beyond our control.

6. One does not always need to invoke God's name to see God's hand at work in our lives.

7. Love your enemies and do good to those who take advantage of you.

# WEEK 3, DAY 4

## Concern for the Oppressed and the Story of God

Whenever we read a biblical text, it is important to ask how the particular text we are reading relates to the rest of the Bible. The themes of concern for the oppressed and loving our enemies have an important place in the story of God. These themes are found in several places in the Bible in a variety of contexts. **In the space provided, write a short summary of how the themes of concern for the oppressed and loving our enemies are discussed in each passage.**

**1. Exodus 23:4–5**

_____

_____

_____

_____

_____

**2. Proverbs 24:17–18**

_____

_____

_____

_____

**3. Jeremiah 7:5–7**

_____

_____

_____

_____

_____

If you have a study Bible, it may have references in a margin, a middle column, or footnotes that point to other biblical texts. You may find it helpful in understanding how the whole story of God ties together to look up some of those other scriptures from time to time.

**4. Zechariah 7:8–10**

_____

_____

_____

_____

_____

_____

_____

_____

**5. Matthew 5:7**

_____

_____

_____

_____

_____

_____

_____

**6. Matthew 5:43–48**

_____

_____

_____

_____

_____

_____

_____

_____

**7. Luke 4:16–21**

**8. Luke 7:27–36**

# WEEK 3, DAY 5

## Esther and Our World Today

When we look at the themes of concern for the oppressed and loving our enemies, they can become the lens through which we see ourselves, our world, and how God works in our world today.

**1. How does the command of God to show mercy to the oppressed affect how we see our world, God's action, and ourselves in our world today?**

Today there are different groups of people who have been marginalized by society and as a result have ended up homeless, lacking access to proper food or water, lacking access to a good education, and living in insecure environments. We may not be able to help everyone, but we can start in our own neighborhoods. Let us look for opportunities to make a difference in individual people's lives.

Following the above example, answer these questions about how we can understand our world, God's action, and ourselves in our world today.

**2. What do you observe about worldly oppression, and how has it affected your life and the lives of your friends?**

_____

_____

_____

_____

_____

_____

**3. We want to protect and support the marginalized in our society. How do we do this in our communities?**

_____

_____

_____

_____

4. The Bible teaches us that we need to love our enemies and do good to those who persecute us. Who are some enemies in your life who need to know that God loves them?

---

---

---

---

---

---

5. What does showing mercy look like today?

---

---

---

---

---

## Invitation and Response

God's Word always invites a response. Think about the way these themes of concern for the oppressed and loving our enemies speak to us today. How do they invite us to respond?

The contrast between Mordecai and Esther's positions is striking. Esther suddenly has a lot of power because she is a queen. Mordecai is an outsider because of his religion, and the king is his enemy, but he shows godly concern for the king anyway. Esther shows us that one can occupy a position of power without discarding their humility or their obligation to care about those whom they rule.

What is your evaluation of yourself based on any or all of the verses in Esther 1–2?

---

---

---

---

---

> One does not always need to invoke God's name to see God's hand at work in our lives.

# ESTHER 3-4

The purpose of our study of Esther 3–4 is to dig more deeply into the story of Esther, her courage in life-and-death issues, Haman's anger issues, and the importance of fasting for special times of seeking God. We may not encounter decisions as significant as Esther's, but we do all have times in our lives when we have to make significant, life-changing decisions. How do we go about doing that? Why does the Bible warn us about anger and its effect on those around us? Haman is a tragic example of uncontrolled and unwarranted anger.

---

## WEEK 4, DAY 1

Listen to the story in Esther 3–4 by reading it aloud several times until you become familiar with the verses, words, and phrases. Observe the character traits and emotions of the people in these chapters.

55

# WEEK 4, DAY 2
## ESTHER 3-4

## The Setting

These chapters continue the story of Esther and introduce the villain Haman, a noble in the service of the Persian king. He is proud, ambitious, and already bothered by Mordecai's lack of deference to him. We learn that Haman is an Amalekite whose tribe is an ancient enemy of the Israelites (see Exodus 17:8–13). This gives us some insight into the ancient conflict between Haman and Mordecai. The mounting anger in Haman results in his plan to get rid of all the Jews in Persia—not just Mordecai.

Mordecai asks Esther to plead for her people, which would require her to go to the king unsummoned. If people do this and the king rejects them, they can face punishment up to and including the death penalty, depending on the king's mood. The tension mounts in the story as we learn that the king has not summoned Esther for some time, and she's been wondering if he has forgotten her or, worse, if she has done something to offend him.

Ultimately, she is the only hope for Jewish salvation. Will she have the courage and creativity to pull off her task?

## The Plot

To discover the plot of Esther 3–4, let us look at the way the writer has structured these chapters. The author introduces Haman and gives us insight into his character flaws. Next, we hear about Haman's plan to get rid of the Jews and thus Mordecai, his archenemy. Mordecai then tells Esther about the plot and shows her she is the only one who can do anything about the situation, suggesting that maybe this is the reason she was made queen.

For the purpose of our study, we divide this passage into six sections. Let us examine each of those six sections. **Below, write down next to each grouping of verses the main theme the verses report, following the examples provided.**

### 1. Esther 3:1–6

The king honors Haman and elevates him to a seat of honor higher than all the other nobles.

All the other officials at the king's gate bow down to Haman, but Mordecai does not. The

officials ask Mordecai why he will not bow down to Haman, and Mordecai tells them it is

because he is a Jew. The officials tell Haman about Mordecai's disrespect to see if Haman will

tolerate it. Haman does not tolerate it. He becomes enraged and turns his anger against not

just Mordecai but all of Mordecai's people.

### 2. Esther 3:7–11

### 3. Esther 3:12–15

## 4. Esther 4:1–8

_____
_____
_____
_____
_____
_____
_____
_____
_____
_____
_____

## 5. Esther 4:9–14

_____
_____
_____
_____
_____
_____
_____
_____
_____
_____
_____

## 6. Esther 4:15–17

Esther commands Mordecai to gather the Jews in Susa to fast for three days. She and her handmaidens fast as well. Then at the end of the three days, she promises to go to the king, unsummoned and against the law. Resigned to her fate, she says, "If I perish, I perish." Mordecai does what Esther has commanded.

# WEEK 4, DAY 3

## What's Happening in the Story?

As we notice certain circumstances in the story, we will begin to see how they are similar to or different from the realities of our world. The story will become the lens through which we see the world in which we live today. In our study today, you may encounter words and/or phrases that are unfamiliar to you. Some of the particular words and translation choices for them have been explained in more detail in the **Word Study Notes**. If you are interested in even more help or detail, you can supplement this study with a Bible dictionary or other Bible study resources.

## 1. Esther 3:1–6

In these verses, the ancient feud between the Jews and Amalekites is fuel added to the fire when the king raises the status of Haman.[1] Mordecai's peers tell Haman that Mordecai is not kneeling down and honoring Haman. Haman does not know Mordecai is not honoring him until the royal officials tell him, and then he becomes enraged. Haman overreacts, deciding to kill all the Jews because of Mordecai's behavior.

## 2. Esther 3:7–11

Haman does not want to leave anything to chance for his revenge, so he looks for divine approval from his gods by casting lots, probably to determine the best day for the massacre.[1] Haman manipulates the king by telling him a partial truth about the Jews—that they have their own laws—implying that they are rebels against his kingdom, which is not true. Haman already has the solution to the problem ready for the king to endorse. The king declines Haman's offer of money[2] but accepts Haman's plan, offering Haman the king's own signet ring as permission.[3]

**WORD STUDY NOTES #1**

[1] Haman is an Amalekite, which we know because 3:1 calls him an Agagite. Agag was a former king of the Amalekite tribe, so if Haman is an Agagite, then he is both an Amalekite and a descendant of the former Amalekite king. The Amalekite tribe is an ancient enemy of the Israelites (see Exodus 17:8-13). This identification of Haman gives us some insight into the ancient conflict between the two tribes to which Haman and Mordecai each belong.

**WORD STUDY NOTES #2**

[1] The grammar in verse 7 is difficult, so scholars are not sure if Haman casts lots to decide which day to present his proposal to the king or which day for the massacre. Casting lots is their way of hearing their gods' will.

[2] The reference to money may indicate that Haman is proposing a bribe.

[3] The signet ring carries the king's symbol. When pressed into wax, it confirms that a document is from the king and carries the king's authority.

## 3. Esther 3:12–15

Haman calls in the scribes and has them write out his edict and translate it into all the languages of the kingdom. The king's seal confirms its authority, and it goes out to all parts of the empire, declaring it to be permissible by law to kill every single Jew, no matter age or gender.[1]

## 4. Esther 4:1–5

When Mordecai finds out about Haman's decree, he very publicly declares his grief—in his clothing, in his weeping, and in the fact that he does it in the public place for political demonstrations, the king's gate.[1] Esther finds out that he is grieving and sends him clothes so he can come into the palace area and tell Esther what is going on. Mordecai refuses to come, and Queen Esther summons one of the king's eunuchs, Hathak, and orders him to find out what is troubling Mordecai.

**Create your own brief description of the world/reality portrayed in Esther 4:6–11 and 4:12–17.**

## 5. Esther 4:6–11[1]

_____

_____

_____

_____

## 6. Esther 4:12–17[1]

_____

_____

_____

_____

_____

## Discoveries

Let's summarize our discoveries from Esther 3–4.

1. Anger that comes from hatred and bitterness will end in violence, whether verbal or physical.

2. God can help us deal with disappointment and evil done to us by giving us his Holy Spirit, who will produce the gifts of the Spirit in us instead of violence.

3. Fasting is one of the spiritual disciplines that can help us focus on important decisions or issues we have to discuss with God.

4. Fasting is not an action to make God do something for us; instead, it is discipline that helps us understand God better and become more like God.

5. Courage is not a lack of fear, but it results in right action in spite of fear.

6. Not all of us may have to make life-and-death choices to be the person God needs us to be, but we should all be willing to die to obey God.

7. While none of us is indispensable to God's plan, we can be a part of bringing the kingdom of heaven to earth if we are willing to carry out God's commands in our lives when God calls us.

If you have a study Bible, it may have references in a margin, a middle column, or footnotes that point to other biblical texts. You may find it helpful in understanding how the whole story of God ties together to look up some of those other scriptures from time to time.

## Obedience and the Story of God

Whenever we read a biblical text, it is important to ask how the particular text we are reading relates to the rest of the Bible. The themes of anger management and obedience have an important place in the story of God. You can find these themes in several places in the Bible and in a variety of contexts. **In the space provided, write a short summary of how the issues of anger management and obedience are discussed in each passage.**

**1. Deuteronomy 28:2**

_____

_____

_____

_____

_____

_____

_____

_____

_____

**2. Psalm 37:8**

_____

_____

_____

_____

_____

_____

_____

_____

_____

_____

### 3. Psalm 119:60

### 4. Ecclesiastes 7:9

### 5. Acts 26:15–19

**6. Romans 12:19**

_____
_____
_____
_____
_____
_____
_____
_____
_____

**7. Ephesians 4:26**

_____
_____
_____
_____
_____
_____
_____
_____
_____

**8. James 1:22**

_____
_____
_____
_____
_____
_____
_____
_____

# WEEK 4, DAY 5

## Esther and Our World Today

When we look at the themes of anger management and obedience in Esther, these themes can become the lens through which we see ourselves, our world, and how God works in our world today..

**1. How does the book of Esther show what happens when human beings are not able to manage their anger? How does uncontrolled anger cause the same type of damage today?**

In these chapters, we see anger boiling up in Haman to the point that he does not just want

revenge on Mordecai but wants to wipe Mordecai's people from the face of the earth. His

uncontrolled rage blinds him. Today, anger often blinds us to a peaceful and just way to solve

a problem.

Following the above example, answer these questions about how we can understand our world, God's action, and ourselves in our world today.

**2. What do you observe about how unmanaged anger has affected your life and the lives of your friends?**

_____

_____

_____

_____

_____

**3. The Bible encourages us to be obedient to God. What does this look like in our modern world?**

_____

_____

_____

_____

_____

4. The Bible teaches us that obedience can be found in how we love our neighbors as ourselves. What are some examples of how we can meet the emotional, physical, social, and spiritual needs of our brothers and sisters in Christ?

_____

_____

_____

_____

_____

5. What is an example of how anger has affected your own community? What could have been done or was done to help manage and direct that anger to bring peace and justice to the community?

_____

_____

_____

_____

_____

## Invitation and Response

God's Word always invites a response. Think about the way these themes of anger management and obedience speak to us today. How does it invite us to respond?

Haman's response to Mordecai invites us to consider the ways that we fail to think and behave rationally when we let anger control our actions. Esther's response to Mordecai invites us to consider the ways we have power that we may not realize, or the ways we can use positions of privilege to help the marginalized.

What is your evaluation of yourself based on any or all of Esther 3–4?

_____

_____

_____

_____

Courage is not a lack of
fear, but it results in right
action in spite of fear.

# ESTHER 5-6

The purpose of our study of Esther 5–6 is to study how cleverness and humility work together in this story to bring about a resolution to the problem of annihilation facing the Jewish people in Persia. Esther is dealing with a narcissistic king who holds the power of life and death over her and her people. Her plan has to work, or the consequences will be horrific! She recognizes that she does not have the wisdom in herself to come up with a plan to save her people. Her humility drives her to ask for God's wisdom and blessing.

## WEEK 5, DAY 1

68

Listen to the story in Esther 5–6 by reading it aloud several times until you become familiar with its verses, words, and phrases. Enjoy the irony of this story when the king forces Haman to honor his archenemy, Mordecai!

# WEEK 5, DAY 2

## ESTHER 5-6

### The Setting

This passage builds on the story as Esther carries out her mission to deliver her people from certain death. Her cleverness and humility will save the day. There are several concepts the original audience for this story would've understood in that culture.

First, Esther bravely stands in the forbidden area of the inner court without being summoned by the king. If the king does not want to see her, he can have her put to death. This is a very high-stakes risk she is taking for herself and her people.

Second, drinking is always an important part of the Persian banquets, and banqueters drink until they are drunk. Note here that it is *after* the banquet, when they are drinking wine, that the king asks Esther what she wants.

Next, hanging an enemy on a pole is meant to make a public show of power over the enemy. The pole represents a place of punishment and a display of power. (There are echoes, here, of Jesus's crucifixion, still yet to come hundreds of years later.)

It was a Persian royal custom to give rewards to people who have done something for the king. In this case, they have neglected to reward Mordecai for saving the king's life, and the king wants it corrected urgently and ostentatiously.

Finally, covering one's face was a custom in the Middle East to indicate grief or shame. Both could describe how Haman is feeling after the king forces him to publicly honor Mordecai.

### The Plot

To discover the plot of Esther 5–6, let us look at the way the writer has structured these chapters. For the purpose of our study, we will divide these chapters into six sections. Let us examine each of those six sections. **In the space provided, write down next to each grouping of verses the main theme the verses report following the examples.**

## 1. Esther 5:1–8

Esther dresses in her royal finery and appears unsummoned before the king in his inner court.

The king warmly welcomes the queen, offering up to half of his kingdom for her request.

Esther invites the king and Haman to a banquet she has prepared for them that day. The king and Haman eat and drink, and the king again offers Esther up to half his kingdom if she will share her request with him. She delays again, and invites both of them to a second banquet the next day.

## 2. Esther 5:9–14

## 3. Esther 6:1–3

## 4. Esther 6:4–9

---

## 5. Esther 6:10–11

---

## 6. Esther 6:12–14

Mordecai goes back to the king's gate after the parade where Haman is forced to publicly praise Mordecai. Haman is humiliated, and rushes home feeling ashamed and aggrieved. Haman's advisers and wife warn him that, because Mordecai is Jewish, Haman cannot stand against him. Immediately, the king's eunuchs come to hurry him to Esther's second banquet.

# WEEK 5, DAY 3

## What's Happening in the Story?

As we notice certain circumstances in the story, we will begin to see how they are similar to or different from the realities of our world. The story will become the lens through which we see the world in which we live today. In our study today, you may encounter words and/or phrases that are unfamiliar to you. Some of the particular words and translation choices for them have been explained in more detail in the **Word Study Notes**. If you are interested in even more help or detail, you can supplement this study with a Bible dictionary or other Bible study resources.

### 1. Esther 5:1–8

In these verses, we see Esther courageously, but not recklessly, carrying out her plan to save her people after her three days of fasting and asking for God's direction and blessing. Dressing in her finest royal robes, she shows that she knows the protocols and appropriate way to dress and behave. She is both cunning and brave. Rather than accepting the offer of half the kingdom, she humbly asks the king and Haman to come to a banquet she has prepared for them. At the appropriate time, when the king invites her to make her petition, Esther asks them to return the next day for another banquet. She is biding her time.

### 2. Esther 5:9–14

**WORD STUDY NOTES #2**

[1] The pole Haman intends to impale Mordecai on is seventy-five feet high—another extreme measure to assuage Haman's fragile ego, like the decision to kill all the Jews.

After being in high spirits, and probably drunk, from Esther's banquet, Haman comes home shaken by the lack of respect Mordecai has shown him, so he calls his friends and his wife together to affirm his worth. He boasts of his wealth, his number of sons, the fact that the king has just promoted him and that he was the only other person besides the king whom Queen Esther invited to her banquet. However, none of this is enough to make him happy. Therefore, his wife proposes that he set up a gigantic pole and ask the king in the morning for permission to impale Mordecai on it. Then Haman can go to his banquet that night and be happy! This idea soothes his bruised ego, and he has the pole set up.[1]

**Write your own brief description of the world and reality portrayed in Esther 6:1–3 and 6:4–9.**

## 3. Esther 6:1–3[1, 2]

_____
_____
_____
_____
_____
_____
_____
_____
_____
_____
_____
_____
_____

## 4. Esther 6:4–9[1]

_____
_____
_____
_____
_____
_____
_____
_____
_____
_____
_____
_____
_____
_____
_____

**WORD STUDY NOTES #3**

[1] The "book of the chronicles" is a record of all the events that have happened in the kingdom. We might liken it to minutes from a meeting or an executive journal that CEOs often keep.

[2] It was customary to thank those who did something for the king—like saving his life!—by rewarding that person.

**WORD STUDY NOTES #4**

[1] It was customary for the king to look for advice from his nobles.

**Write your own brief description of the world and reality portrayed in Esther 6:10-11.**

## 5. Esther 6:10–11

_____

_____

_____

_____

_____

_____

_____

_____

_____

_____

_____

_____

_____

_____

_____

**WORD STUDY NOTES #6**

[1] There is a full reversal of fortunes here with Haman being the one who runs from the scene with his head covered, indicating deep grief and humiliation.

[2] Here we see implied the fear and awareness of the power of the Jewish God that was common knowledge at the time.

## 6. Esther 6:12–14

Haman flees the scene after the humiliation of the public parade. We are told he covers his head in grief,[1] but of course we know he is also probably enraged. Haman hears from his wife and advisers the ominous warning that, since Mordecai is Jewish, there is no way Haman can win against him![2] Before he can process this, the eunuchs come to hurry him away to Queen Esther's banquet.

## Discoveries

Let's summarize our discoveries from Esther 5–6.

1. Doing the right thing can be dangerous and life-threatening. It is important to know your context and behave in a way that will minimize the possibility of failure.

2. There is nothing wrong with careful planning and strategizing to get the results you need. Just winging it and hoping for the best is not necessarily the Christian thing to do.

3. We need to learn to live in the joy and abundance of the blessings God has given us, and not fixate on the one thing we do not have. This is the secret to living without jealousy.

4. We may see the acts of God in the everyday happenings in our lives. Sometimes it takes awhile, so we often see God's hand when we look back on our lives.

5. Occasionally, we see God directly at work in our lives as doors open and circumstances move us in the direction of God's choosing. However, we should never attribute anything in the process to God that is contrary to God's nature.

6. True humility is seeing ourselves as God sees us, not thinking of ourselves as worthless.

7. Honor is not something that comes from our trying to make others think we are honorable. Honor comes from within and is found in a Christlike character.

If you have a study Bible, it may have references in a margin, a middle column, or footnotes that point to other biblical texts. You may find it helpful in understanding how the whole story of God ties together to look up some of those other scriptures from time to time.

## Cleverness, Humility, and the Story of God

Whenever we read a biblical text, it is important to ask how the particular text we are reading relates to the rest of the Bible. The themes of cunning and humility have an important place in the story of God. We can find these themes in several places in the Bible and in a variety of contexts. In the Old and New Testaments, the themes of cunning and humility are common. The Bible often gives direction and advice on right action to God's people. **In the space provided, write a short summary of how cleverness or humility are revealed in each passage.**

**1. Psalm 131:1**

_____

_____

_____

_____

_____

_____

_____

_____

**2. Proverbs 12:18**

_____

_____

_____

_____

_____

_____

_____

**3. Proverbs 22:4**

**4. Ecclesiastes 8:5**

**5. Matthew 10:16**

**6. Matthew 23:11–12**

_____
_____
_____
_____
_____
_____
_____
_____
_____

**7. Philippians 2:3**

_____
_____
_____
_____
_____
_____
_____
_____

**8. Colossians 4:5**

_____
_____
_____
_____
_____
_____
_____

# WEEK 5, DAY 5

## Esther and Our World Today

When we look at the themes of cleverness and humility in Esther, these themes can become the lens through which we see our world, ourselves, and how God works in our world today.

**1. How does the revelation that God does bless strategic planning affect how we see our world, God's action, and ourselves in our world today?**

We realize that God expects us to use our God-given ability to think and strategize for his glory. There is a difference between manipulation and strategy. Manipulation's purpose is to deceive. Strategy's purpose is to take all aspects of the context and situation into consideration to accomplish a worthy goal.

**Following the above example, answer these questions about how we can understand our world, God's action, and ourselves in our world today.**

**2. What do you observe about how jealousy (yours or your neighbor's) has affected your life and the lives of your friends?**

**3. We want to have a mature faith that is evidenced by godly wisdom. What might this look like in our modern world?**

**4. The Bible teaches us that God blesses the humble. What does it mean to be humble in our society?**

_____

_____

_____

_____

_____

**5. What is the difference between godly humility and low self-esteem?**

_____

_____

_____

_____

_____

## Invitation and Response

God's Word always invites a response. Think about the way the themes of cleverness and humility in Esther speak to us today. How do they invite us to respond?

Esther's story invites us to consider the ways that we can use our brains and our logic for the

mission of God. While the phrase "God helps those who helps themselves" is not biblical and

not something we should tout, it hints at the grain of truth that God did equip us with brains

and the ability to think and reason, which means that God expects and intends us to use our

brains in the unique ways they are wired. Esther's story encourages us to think about how we

can follow God's guidance of our thinking and our creativity in order to humbly advance God's

kingdom, rather than coming up with self-serving schemes that may be clever but serve and

love no one.

What is your evaluation of yourself based on any or all of Esther 5–6?

_____

_____

_____

True humility is seeing ourselves as God sees us, not thinking of ourselves as worthless.

# ESTHER 7-8

The purpose of our study of Esther 7–8 is to study the continuing faithfulness of God and how that is reflected in our own godly vocation. This section begins with Queen Esther's courageous confrontation and accusation of genocide by Haman, followed by Haman's demise and Mordecai's rise to power. Here God reveals his faithfulness in the living out of Esther's calling and Mordecai's vocation. Chapter 8 ends with the reversal of the evil and violent plans of Haman to have the Jews annihilated.

---

## WEEK 6, DAY 1

82

Listen to the story in Esther 7–8 by reading it aloud several times until you become familiar with its verses, words, and phrases. Enjoy hearing how hope returns to God's people in Persia after experiencing a time of utter despair and grief.

# WEEK 6, DAY 2

## ESTHER 7-8

## The Setting

As chapter 7 opens, the king and Haman are at Esther's banquet. The king again asks Esther for her request. She makes a direct request that her life and the lives of her people be spared. The king asks who has threatened her life, and she accuses Haman. The king's response is swift and decisive, ending with the king's order to impale Haman on the pole he set up for Mordecai.

Chapter 8 is the story of the attempt to reverse the damage Haman has done with the edict to kill the Jews. Since the law cannot be reversed, Mordecai writes another edict, with the king's permission, that allows the Jews to defend themselves. This new edict brings joy and relief to the Jewish people, and the gentiles now fear the Jews, which can be read as fear of the Jewish God.

## The Plot

To discover the plot of Esther 7-8, let us look at the way the writer structured the passage. For the purpose of our study, we will divide these chapters into seven sections. Let us examine each of those sections. **Below, write down next to each grouping of verses the main theme the verses report following the examples provided.**

**1. Esther 7:1-6**

The king and Haman come to the banquet Esther has prepared for them the second night. The king again invites Queen Esther to share with him her petition. Esther asks the king to spare her life and the lives of her people. The king asks who is threatening her life, and she points out Haman. Haman is terrified.

**2. Esther 7:7-8**

_____

_____

_____

_____

_____

### 3. Esther 7:9–10

_____

_____

_____

_____

_____

_____

_____

_____

### 4. Esther 8:1–2

_____

_____

_____

_____

_____

_____

_____

_____

### 5. Esther 8:3–8

_____

_____

_____

_____

_____

_____

_____

## 6. Esther 8:9-14

## 7. Esther 8:15–17

Mordecai leaves the king's presence wearing royal robes and a large crown. The city of Susa

has a celebration. It is a time of joy, feasting, and celebration throughout the whole empire.

Many non-Jews convert to Judaism out of fear, and to keep themselves safe.

# WEEK 6, DAY 3

## What's Happening in the Story?

As we notice certain circumstances in the story, we will begin to see how they are similar to or different from the realities of our world. The story will become the lens through which we see the world in which we live today. In our study today, you may encounter words and/or phrases that are unfamiliar to you. Some of the particular words and translation choices for them have been explained in more detail in the **Word Study Notes**. If you are interested in even more help or detail, you can supplement this study with a Bible dictionary or other Bible study resources.

**WORD STUDY NOTES #1**

[1] The last phrase of verse 4 is ambiguous in the Hebrew, and you can read both options in the NIV. The ambiguity might be purposeful, but the king seems to understand the second interpretation about the money.

## 1. Esther 7:1-6

At the second banquet, Esther makes her request of the king, completing her ultimate purpose in life. Her life, up to this point, has been a preparation for her request to save her people. This is the moment of finishing her task but also the most vulnerable moment in her life. Esther elaborates on her simple request in verse 3 by emphasizing the monetary nature of the destruction of her people.[1] She uses three words to describe the horrific implications of Haman's edict: "destroyed, killed, and annihilated." The king is alarmed by the prospect of losing income and asks for the identity of Esther's adversary. When Haman is identified, he rightly becomes terrified.

## 2. Esther 7:7-8

Here the fate of Haman is sealed in a series of events that happen simultaneously. The king is angry that Haman has duped him into destroying the people who include his queen. Haman falls on Esther's couch, pleading for his life just when the king comes back into the room. Haman's compromising position gives the king another reason to end Haman's life.

**Practice the pattern to jot down a summary description of the reality that is portrayed in Esther 7:9–10.**

## 3. Esther 7:9–10[1]

_____

_____

_____

_____

_____

_____

_____

**WORD STUDY NOTES #3**

[1] The king's advisor supplies the king with a plan to get rid of Haman, making sure the king knows that the pole Haman set up was intended for Mordecai, who saved the king's life.

## 4. Esther 8:1–2

The king gives Haman's[1] estate to Queen Esther, and she then reveals her relationship to Mordecai, whom the king already knows is Jewish. The king gives his signet ring to Mordecai, making him the most important noble in the kingdom,[2] and Esther puts Mordecai in charge of Haman's estate. Therefore, the reversal of fortunes and status is now complete between Haman and Mordecai.

**Create your own brief description of the world/reality portrayed in Esther 8:3-8 and 8:9-14.**

**WORD STUDY NOTES #4**

[1] Haman's name is followed by the label "enemy of the Jews," indicating that this whole conflict and story is the age-old story of God's protection of his people against their enemies.

[2] The signet ring is the symbol of the favor and delegated power of the king to those to whom he gives it.

## 5. Esther 8:3–8[1, 2]

_____

_____

_____

_____

_____

_____

**WORD STUDY NOTES #5**

[1] Esther is courageously asking the king to overrule the edict sent out by Haman. The tradition is that no one, not even the king, can overrule a law of the Medes and Persians.

[2] The full titles of King Xerxes and Queen Esther are given in verse seven, indicating an official statement.

[1] Here the edict favoring the Jews follows the exact same procedures as the one ordered by Haman.

[2] The violent language in verse 11 is disconcerting. One way to understand it is as a mirrored reversal of the theme of destruction that has pervaded the whole story. But there is a subtle difference in that the Jewish violence is only in self-defense.

## 6. Esther 8:9–14[1, 2]

_____

_____

_____

_____

_____

_____

_____

_____

_____

_____

_____

88

## 7. Esther 8:15–17

Here we see Mordecai given the rank and honor of Haman. The Jews from the city of Susa and on out to all the provinces rejoice. Many non-Jews convert because they have seen the power of the Jewish God.

_____

_____

_____

_____

_____

_____

_____

_____

_____

## Discoveries

Let's summarize our discoveries from Esther 7–8.

1. God will act on our behalf, but we must also fulfill our own calling.

2. God's judgment can come quickly to those who are disobedient.

3. We can always count on God to be faithful to God's people, even in the darkest of days.

4. The vocation or calling on our lives requires us to be the people God created us to be, even if it looks like "the other side" is winning.

5. Fulfilling our call is not always easy. Sometimes it requires us to stand up for what is right even when that might mean our own loss of power, honor, or life.

6. God's faithfulness to God's people usually requires the interaction of God's people in the process of fulfilling God's will.

7. Standing up for what is right does not mean one needs to be obnoxious and uncivilized in the process.

If you have a study Bible, it may have references in a margin, a middle column, or footnotes that point to other biblical texts. You may find it helpful in understanding how the whole story of God ties together to look up some of those other scriptures from time to time.

## Our Calling and the Story of God

Whenever we read a biblical text, it is important to ask how the particular text we are reading relates to the rest of the Bible. The themes of God's faithfulness and our vocation have an important place in the story of God. We find these themes in several places in the Bible and in a variety of contexts. **In the space provided, write a short summary of how the themes of God's faithfulness or human vocation are revealed in each passage.**

**1. Deuteronomy 28:9–10**

_____

_____

_____

_____

_____

_____

_____

_____

**2. 1 Samuel 3:8–10**

_____

_____

_____

_____

_____

_____

_____

_____

**3. 1 Kings 8:20**

**4. Psalm 117:2**

**5. Romans 8:28**

**6. Philippians 3:14**

_____
_____
_____
_____
_____
_____
_____
_____
_____

**7. 2 Timothy 2:11–13**

_____
_____
_____
_____
_____
_____
_____
_____

**8. Hebrews 10:23–25**

_____
_____
_____
_____
_____
_____
_____
_____
_____

# WEEK 6, DAY 5

## Esther and Our World Today

When we look at the themes of the faithfulness of God and human calling in Esther, these themes can become the lens through which we see our world, ourselves, and how God works in our world today.

**1. How does the revelation that God does place a call on our lives affect how we see our world, God's action, and ourselves in our world today?**

This story in Esther suggests that, as God's people, we are obligated to actively participate in

making the world a better place—a place that God desires to dwell. We are participants in

bringing about God's kingdom on earth.

Following the above example, answer these questions about how we can understand ourselves, our world, and God's action in our world today.

**2. How has the faithfulness of God affected your life and the lives of your friends?**

**3. How do you see God's calling on your life? How is it related to your current job, or how does it show up in other ways?**

**4. The Bible teaches us in multiple different places that God will be faithful even if we are not faithful to God. How have you experienced God's faithfulness in your life?**

_____

_____

_____

**5. The Bible tells us that if we know God wants us to do something and we do not do it, it is sin (see James 4:17). Thinking about that truth as it relates to Esther's story, how does that affect our thinking about God's call on our lives?**

_____

_____

_____

_____

_____

## Invitation and Response

God's Word always invites a response. Think about the way the themes of God's faithfulness and our calling or vocation speak to us today. How do they invite us to respond?

Esther's story invites us to consider what purpose God might have for our lives, and how we

might mirror God's faithfulness by being faithful to God in response to God's calling.

_____

What is your evaluation of yourself based on any or all of Esther 7–8?

_____

_____

_____

_____

_____

_____

Fulfilling our call may require us to stand up for what is right even when that might mean our own loss of power, honor, or life.

# ESTHER 9–10

The purpose of our study of Esther 9–10 is to understand the nature of salvation history (that is, God's acts of salvation within history) and our partnership with God. When God and God's people work together, Haman's original plan is turned on its head, and the Jewish people—primarily identified here in the person of Mordecai—become more and more powerful.

## WEEK 7, DAY 1

Listen to the story in Esther 9–10 by reading it aloud several times until you become familiar with its verses, words, and phrases. Enjoy hearing the abundant fulfillment of God's promises to the Jews living in the foreign land of the Persian empire. Here we have a telling of salvation history and the partnership of God's people with God in bringing about their salvation.

# WEEK 7, DAY 2

## ESTHER 9–10

## The Setting

These chapters are the triumphant climax of a story that is full of intrigue, danger, and political manipulation. Chapter 9 begins on the day Haman chose, through a casting of lots, for the annihilation of the Jews, but because of Esther and Mordecai's influence, the Jews are now allowed to defend themselves, so they assemble and organize all over the Persian empire to defend themselves and kill as many of their enemies as possible.

The reports of those killed are all enemies of the Jews, and there are no reports of Persians killing any Jews. Seventy-five thousand enemies of the Jews are reported killed on the first day, with three hundred more killed in Susa on the second day.

The violence described in chapter 9 is repulsive to our modern sensibilities, but it is not unusual in its context. The numbers given express how great a victory the Jews have and, in a way, those numbers show the greatness of God. A couple of things are important to understand. One is that this is a kill-or-be-killed situation, and the Jews kill out of self-defense. The other is that, while they kill their enemies, they do not plunder their homes even though the second edict says they can.

In the last part of chapter 9, we learn that the story of the book of Esther has been told as the background story to the Festival of Purim—the story of God's deliverance in Persia, much like the story in the book of Exodus tells us the background behind the Festival of Passover.

Chapter 10 is very short, establishing Mordecai's high rank in the kingdom, second only to the king. The reason for God's blessing on his life is that he has worked for the good of his people and spoken up for their welfare. Here is an example for all diaspora Jews (those living outside Palestine) to follow. They can be great in non-Jewish nations if they are willing to stand up for their own people and work with God for their protection.

## The Plot

To discover the plot of Esther 9–10, let us look at the way the writer structured this passage. For the purpose of our study, we will divide these chapters into seven sections. Let us examine each of those sections. **Write down next to each grouping of verses the main theme of the passage, following the examples provided.**

### 1. Esther 9:1–4

The thirteenth day of Adar is the day the enemies of the Jews hoped to overpower them, but the tables are turned because the second edict has given the Jews permission to organize and defend themselves. The other nationalities are afraid of the Jews. The nobles, governors, and the king's administrators help the Jews because Mordecai's prominence and power have grown throughout the whole Persian empire.

### 2. Esther 9:5–10

### 3. Esther 9:11–15

## 4. Esther 9:16–19

_____

_____

_____

_____

_____

_____

## 5. Esther 9:20–28

_____

_____

_____

_____

_____

_____

## 6. Esther 9:29–32

_____

_____

_____

_____

_____

_____

_____

## 7. Esther 10:1–3

King Xerxes gathers tributes (or taxes) from even the most distant of his provinces. The king's

power and the greatness of Mordecai are written in the annals of the kings of Media and

Persia. Mordecai is second-in-command to King Xerxes and is held in high regard because he

has worked for the good of his people and spoken up for their welfare.

## What's Happening in the Story?

As we notice certain circumstances in the story, we will begin to see how they are similar to or different from the realities of our world. The story will become the lens through which we see the world in which we live today. In our study today, you may encounter words and/or phrases that are unfamiliar to you. Some of the particular words and translation choices for them have been explained in more detail in the **Word Study Notes**. If you are interested in even more help or detail, you can supplement this study with a Bible dictionary or other Bible study resources.

**WORD STUDY NOTES #1**

[1] This is significant because it establishes the dates for the future Festival of Purim.

[2] In the book of Esther we find several references to the other nationalities in Persia being afraid of the Jews or afraid of Mordecai. What we need to understand here is that their fear is actually of the Jewish God because God is the one who has given power and victory to the Jews.

[3] The text names the nobles, satraps, governors, and administrators to show that the ruling class understands whose side their king is on. So, even though Haman's edict has riled up the commoners, the government is instructed to help the Jews defend themselves.

## 1. Esther 9:1–4

This chapter opens with giving the exact date of the planned battle between the other nationalities and the Jews, based on the original edict that Haman sent out with the king's authority.[1] It also says that the Jews have assembled to attack those who are "determined to destroy them." Therefore, while it appears that the Jews might be aggressors here, they have assembled only to defend themselves. They do not see themselves as the ones who started the fight. Nevertheless, the text says that the other nationalities, while wanting to destroy the Jews, are also afraid of them.[2] The ruling class of Persia has seen the power of God in Mordecai, and they want to be on the right side of history![3] Because of his obedience, God has blessed Mordecai with prominence in the palace and a reputation of political power and favor with the king throughout all the provinces.

**Practice the pattern to jot down a summary description of the reality that is portrayed in Esther 9:5–10.**

## 2. Esther 9:5–10[1, 2, 3, 4]

_____

_____

_____

_____

_____

_____

_____

_____

_____

_____

_____

_____

_____

## 3. Esther 9:11–15

The governing officials keep the king informed of the progress of the Jews in defending themselves, and he is in constant contact with Queen Esther to make sure that what she wanted done is happening. When Esther sees that only the enemies in the walled city have been killed on the first day, she asks for a second day of fighting to be allowed so the enemies in the surrounding city of the common people might be killed.[1] She cares about all the Jews, whether of elite or common status. To reinforce the fact that Jews are not be to harmed, she asks for the bodies of Haman's sons to be displayed on poles, showing the absolute victory and power of the Jews—and, thus, the Jewish God.[2] Esther's wish is granted by the king's edict. The Jews were not interested in looting the homes of their enemies, indicating that their purpose is self-defense and not aggression or vengeance.[3]

**WORD STUDY NOTES #2**

[1] The history of killing all their enemies goes back to the long-standing animosity between the Amalekites (Haman's people) and the Israelites, which began shortly after Israel crossed the Red Sea (Exodus 17), and continued in the significant battle between the two during King Saul's rule. God commanded Saul (1 Samuel 15:3) to totally destroy the Amalekites because of their attack on the Israelites after they left Egypt. The Hebrew word (herem) is the term for total destruction and was common in that age and culture for any conquering group of people. Saul did not obey God; thus, we have the Amalekites raising their heads again in an attempt to annihilate the Jews in Persia.

[2] The city of Susa consisted of a walled city that protected the palace and the homes of the elite.

[3] The text names the ten sons of Haman to emphasize the total destruction of Haman's family.

[4] The comment on plunder indicates that they are not taking vengeance on Haman's family to gain from their wealth but are obeying God's original command to completely destroy the Amalekites.

**WORD STUDY NOTES #3**

[1] Esther's request for a second day of fighting in the city of Susa indicates that, the first day, the fighting was only within the walled city and with the elite Persians. The second day is to fight the enemies of the Jews in the city of the common people outside Susa's walled city.

[2] They kill Haman's sons on the first day but impale them on the second day. In this case, the pole is not a method of execution but a display of the bodies of the most heinous of the enemies. This was a common practice in the culture and should not be taken as exceptionally harsh.

[3] The phrase "they did not lay their hands on the plunder" shows both obedience to God and restraint on the part of the victorious Jews.

**Create your own brief description of the world/reality portrayed in Esther 9:16–19 and 9:20–23.**

## 4. Esther 9:16–19[1]

_____

_____

_____

_____

_____

_____

_____

_____

## 5. Esther 9:20–23

_____

_____

_____

_____

_____

_____

_____

## 6. Esther 9:24–26a

These verses summarize what has happened in the book of Esther, explaining that Haman cast the lot to determine the date for the ruin and destruction of the Jews. It is possible that this emphasis on Haman's casting implies that the God of the Jews was actually the one determining the auspicious day, giving time for discovery, response, and preparation on the part of the Jews to be able to defend themselves. The festival is called Purim (the plural of _pur_) precisely because of the casting of lots.[1]

**Write your own brief description of the world and reality portrayed in Esther 9:26b–28.**

## 7. Esther 9:26b-28

_____

_____

_____

_____

_____

_____

_____

_____

_____

_____

_____

## 8. Esther 9:29–32

Here we have the official announcement and confirmation of Queen Esther's involvement in sending a second letter to the Jews in all 127 provinces of the kingdom to establish the Festival of Purim as well as the regulations on how to celebrate this annual festival. In Esther, we see the development of salvation history, since now the Jews are spread out throughout the country of Persia instead of being a nation that is fighting specifically against another nation. The Jews' well-being also brings well-being to the people they live with. We see that God's agents of change are not just men, and not just the lowly, but also include women and men in positions of power.

## 9. Esther 10:1–3

This postscript shows that the king's decision to listen to Esther and Mordecai results in financial benefit for the kingdom and in the king being even more powerful than he was before. It also confirms Mordecai's position as second-in-command of the Persian empire because he spoke up and protected his own people.

## Discoveries

Let's summarize our discoveries from Esther 9–10.

1. God's protection of God's people requires obedience by God's people. In their obedience, they find victory over their problems.

2. When God calls us to do something we see as difficult, we can be sure that God will be there to guide and empower us.

3. When God gives us victory over our enemies, we are not to gloat or take advantage of their defeat. God loves all of God's creation.

4. God's plan of salvation was to bless the whole world through God's chosen people. They are to be a light to the nations and a bridge between the nations and God.

5. God's calling extends to both women and men, who are expected to partner with one another and with God in the fulfilling of God's plans for creation.

6. Help to overcome our problems can come from unlikely places. We should be alert and ready to collaborate with those who want to do the will of God.

7. We should write down and remember the spiritual victories in our personal and community lives. The next time we face adversity in living for God, the memory of God's help in the past will be an encouragement for us to continue to trust and believe in God.

# WEEK 7, DAY 4

## Salvation History and the Story of God

Whenever we read a biblical text, it is important to ask how the particular text we are reading relates to the rest of the Bible. The themes of salvation history and partnership with God have an important place in the story of God. We find these themes in several places in the Bible and in a variety of contexts. **In the space provided, write a short summary of how the themes of salvation history or partnership with God are discussed in each passage.**

**1. Ezra 1:2–4**

_____

_____

_____

_____

_____

_____

_____

**2. Isaiah 12:2**

_____

_____

_____

_____

_____

_____

_____

If you have a study Bible, it may have references in a margin, a middle column, or footnotes that point to other biblical texts. You may find it helpful in understanding how the whole story of God ties together to look up some of those other scriptures from time to time.

105

**3. Jeremiah 31:33**

_____

_____

_____

_____

_____

_____

_____

_____

**4. Lamentations 3:25–26**

_____

_____

_____

_____

_____

_____

_____

_____

**5. Romans 3:21–24**

_____

_____

_____

_____

_____

_____

_____

_____

_____

_____

**6. Romans 16:1–5**

_____

_____

_____

_____

_____

_____

_____

_____

_____

**7. 1 Corinthians 3:6–9**

_____

_____

_____

_____

_____

_____

_____

_____

**8. Hebrews 9:27–28**

_____

_____

_____

_____

_____

_____

_____

_____

_____

_____

# WEEK 7, DAY 5

## Esther and Our World Today

When we look at the themes of salvation history and partnership with God in Esther, these themes can become the lens through which we see ourselves, our world, and how God works in our world today.

**1. How does the revelation that God is willing to work with a gentile king, as well as with both men and women of God, affect how we see our world, God's action, and ourselves in our world today?**

We should be willing to work with anyone who wants to bring about peace and restoration in

our world. God's people do not have a monopoly on the ideas and resources to bring about

peace and the restoration of right relationship between God and creation. There are others

willing to partner with us for a righteous purpose.

**Following the previous example, answer these questions about how we can understand ourselves, our world, and God's action in our world today.**

**2. The book of Esther shows that God cares about God's people when they are being persecuted and harassed by ungodly people. How does this knowledge affect your life and the lives of your friends?**

_____

_____

_____

_____

**3. As we think back on Esther's reliance on prayer and fasting (not just her own, but also the prayers and fasting of her entire community) to give her the courage and wisdom to deal with a difficult situation, how does that affect how you view your prayer life and the prayers of others for you?**

_____

_____

_____

_____

4. Esther was written to remind the Jewish people of God's deliverance from their enemies in Persia. They were to celebrate this victory annually. How can we remember God's deliverance and victories in our own lives and in the church community? What might that look like in our modern world?

_____

_____

_____

_____

5. Esther and Mordecai were called to partner with each other. They had different gifts and abilities that God needed to bring about the salvation of the Jews. What do we learn from this about how God intends for men and women to work together for God's kingdom?

_____

_____

_____

_____

## Invitation and Response

God's Word always invites a response. Think about the way the themes of salvation history and partnership with God and others speak to us today. How do they invite us to respond?

Esther's story invites us to consider the ways we can be in partnership with unexpected people

we find ourselves surrounded with. It urges us to take a look at those who are nearby, and

pray for God's guidance about how we can partner with them to advance God's kingdom.

What is your evaluation of yourself based on any or all of Esther 9–10?

_____

_____

_____

_____

When God calls us to do something we
see as difficult, we can be sure that God
will be there to guide and empower us.